THE MERCHANT OF VENICE

Stephen Rickard

Illustrated by Alina Soare

Ransom

The Merchant of Venice
Published by Ransom Publishing Ltd.
Unit 7, Brocklands Farm, West Meon, Hampshire GU32 1JN, UK
www.ransom.co.uk

ISBN   978 178591 336 5
First published in 2019

CONTENTS

WHERE

The action takes place mostly in **Venice**, a city in Italy, and in Belmont. We aren't told where Belmont is, but it cannot be too far from Venice.

Padua

Venice

Padua, a small town in Italy, is also mentioned.

ITALY

THE MICROWAVE
Shakespeare

Other titles in the series

WHEN

The Merchant of Venice was probably written between 1596 and 1599.

We don't know exactly when the events in the play take place.

WHO

Antonio – a merchant

Bassanio – a gentleman of Venice and friend of Antonio

Gratiano – friend of Bassanio

Antonio

Bassanio

Gratiano

Portia – a wealthy heiress from Belmont

Shylock – a Jewish moneylender in Venice

Shylock   Portia

Salarino – friend of Antonio and Bassanio

Salanio – friend of Antonio and Bassanio

Lorenzo – friend of Antonio and Bassanio

Salerio – a Venetian gentleman and merchant

Nerissa – Portia's lady-in-waiting

Balthazar – servant of Portia

> (Later in the play Portia disguises herself
> as a lawyer from Rome. She uses the
> name of her servant, **Balthazar**, for
> this lawyer.)

The Prince of Morocco – suitor to Portia
The Prince of Arragon – suitor to Portia

Doctor Bellario – a wealthy lawyer from
Padua. Portia's cousin

A messenger – a lawyer's clerk supposedly
sent by Bellario. The messenger is in fact
Nerissa in disguise

Jessica – Shylock's daughter

The Duke of Venice – ruler of Venice

Tubal – a wealthy Jew and friend of Shylock

Launcelot Gobbo – a servant
Stephano – a messenger
Leonardo – servant of Bassanio

HELPFUL NOTE

All the spoken words in this book that are
in italics, *'like this'*, are actual words taken
from Shakespeare's play. They are spoken
by one of the actors in the play.

The Globe Theatre. Above is a reconstruction of the original Globe Theatre, which is in London. Below is a cross-section of the original theatre, which was built in 1599.

Shakespeare's plays were performed at this theatre. When you read this book, just imagine standing in the crowd, in front of this stage, watching the play.

ONE

In a street in Venice, the merchant **Antonio** is with his friends **Salarino** and **Salanio**. Antonio is sad. His friends tell him it's because his ships are in peril on the high seas.

'No,' says Antonio. 'I'm rich. My business affairs don't make me sad.'

'You're in love, then,' Salanio tells him.

'No way.'

Then Antonio's friends **Bassanio**, **Lorenzo** and **Gratiano** turn up.

'You don't look well,' Gratiano tells Antonio. 'You're taking everything too seriously.'

'*I hold the world but as the world, Gratiano;*
A stage where every man must play a part,
And mine a sad one,' replies Antonio.
Nope, he's not in a good mood.

'Cheer up,' says Gratiano. 'I'd rather be
happy than glum any day.' Gratiano
goes on for a bit (he's a bit of a windbag)
and then he leaves. 'See you later!'

'Is Gratiano right?' Antonio asks Bassanio.

'*Gratiano speaks an infinite deal of nothing,*
more than any man in all Venice,' Bassanio
replies.

But Bassanio has his own problems, too. He owes money to various people, including Antonio, and he's very keen to get all his debts paid off.

'When I was a kid, sometimes I fired an arrow and couldn't find where it went,' Bassanio explains. 'But if I fired a second arrow in the same direction, and watched it carefully, sometimes I'd find both the first arrow and the second. So risking a second arrow often got me both arrows back.'

Bassanio asks Antonio to help him fire a second arrow – in other words, to lend Bassanio more money, so he can clear all of his debts.

'There's a girl I know,' Bassanio explains. 'Her name is **Portia**. She is beautiful and good, and she's inherited a lot of money. I think she likes me. She's got lots of suitors, but if I had the money to hold them off, I know I could win her.'

Antonio tells Bassanio he'd be very happy to lend him the money, as a friend, but he hasn't got any. He's rich, but all his money is tied up in his ships at sea. 'But why don't you use my credit in Venice to borrow money,' he says to Bassanio. 'I'll guarantee whatever you borrow. *Try what my credit can in Venice do.*'

Meanwhile in Belmont, Portia is at home with her maid, **Nerissa**. Portia tells Nerissa she is *'aweary of this great world.'*

Portia needs to choose a husband, but she is bound to follow instructions her father left in his will. Her father instructed that any man wanting to marry Portia must choose one of three caskets (or boxes) – one made of lead, one of silver and one of gold. The man who picks the right casket gets to marry Portia.

'Do you like any of the suitors you've seen so far?' asks Nerissa. 'First there was that prince from Naples … '

'All he talks about is his horse. I think his mother must have had an affair with a blacksmith,' interrupts Portia.

'Then there's that Count Palatine … '
Nerissa continues.

'He never smiles. *I had rather be married to a death's-head with a bone in his mouth than to either of these.*'

Nerissa carries on through the list of suitors, but none of them are acceptable to Portia. Which is OK, because none of the suitors want to take the casket test anyway.

'There was that Bassanio character, the Venetian scholar and soldier,' says Portia. 'He wasn't bad … '

Back in Venice, Bassanio has taken up Antonio's offer. He is trying to borrow money from the Jewish moneylender **Shylock**.

'Three thousand ducats for three months,' says Bassanio. 'And Antonio will guarantee the loan. So if I don't repay it to you, he will. What do you say?'

Shylock thinks he can do it, but he needs

to speak to Antonio first, just to be sure
that he will guarantee it.

Then Antonio turns up. Good timing!

Shylock does not like Antonio. To himself,
Shylock says:

'I hate him for he is a Christian,
But more for that in low simplicity
He lends out money gratis and brings down
The rate of usance here with us in Venice.'

Part of Shylock's problem with Antonio is
that Antonio lends money to others without

charging them interest. That means that, as a moneylender, Shylock has to charge less interest on his loans. So Antonio's generosity is costing Shylock money.

Shylock also thinks that Antonio hates Jews. 'If I can catch him once, I'll satisfy my *ancient grudge* against him,' he says.

Antonio tells Shylock that he doesn't usually borrow money if he has to pay interest on the loan, but he will do it this time to help his friend Bassanio. So, Antonio asks, will Shylock lend Bassanio the money?

'Antonio, you've often insulted my money and my business of lending,' replies Shylock, 'but I have *borne it with a patient shrug*

For sufferance is the badge of all our tribe [he means the Jewish people]. You call me a heathen and a *cut-throat dog.* You spit on my Jewish clothes. And all because I use that which is mine to earn money. And *it now appears you need my help.* Now you come to me to borrow money.'

Antonio doesn't deny anything Shylock

says. 'I'll probably call you those things again,' he says to Shylock. 'So if you're going to lend us the money, don't lend it to us as if we were friends. Lend it to me as your enemy. Then, if I default on the loan, it's easier for you to take the penalty.'

'OK, here's my offer,' says Shylock. 'I'll lend you the money – with no interest. You must repay me three months from today. And, *in a merry sport*, if you don't repay me on the day it's due, then I can take *an equal pound*

Of your fair flesh, to be cut off and taken
In what part of your body pleaseth me.'

'Agreed,' says Antonio. 'And I'll even say that Jews are nice, as part of the deal.'

Bassanio's not happy with the pound of flesh bit, but Antonio assures him there won't be a problem.

So the deal is done and Bassanio gets his money.

What could possibly go wrong?

TWO

Back at Portia's house in Belmont, Portia is meeting another suitor – the **Prince of Morocco**. She tells him that he still needs to pass the casket test but, from her point of view, '*Yourself, renowned prince, then stood as fair*
As any comer I have look'd on yet
For my affection.'

'Bring on the casket test,' says the prince.

'You must take your chance,' says Portia. 'You don't have to choose, but if you do, and if you get it wrong, you must swear never to speak to any woman again about getting married.'

That's a tough condition for anyone to agree to!

'Bring it on,' says the prince.

In a street in Venice, Shylock's servant **Launcelot Gobbo** is debating whether he should stop working for his master or not. *'Certainly the Jew is the very devil incarnal,'* he says. 'But should I run?'

Then Bassanio turns up, and Launcelot asks Bassanio if he might work for him. 'I spoke to Shylock today,' says Bassanio, 'and he suggested you to me. So yes, Launcelot, you can come and work for me.'

Then Gratiano catches up with Bassanio. Bassanio now has the money he borrowed from Shylock, and he's planning to visit Portia at her home in Belmont.

Gratiano asks Bassanio if he can go with him to Belmont. Bassanio replies with some words of advice for his friend. *'Gratiano; Thou art too wild, too rude and bold of voice.*

That's OK with us, because we are your friends and we know you. But in places where they don't know you, you need to be quieter and more serious. Because otherwise *thy skipping spirit* will ruin my chances with Portia.'

Gratiano promises to behave, so Bassanio agrees that he can accompany him.

At Shylock's house, Shylock's daughter **Jessica** is saying goodbye to Launcelot, as he leaves to join Bassanio's household. She gives Launcelot a letter to give to Lorenzo.

As Launcelot leaves, Jessica thinks aloud:
'Alack, *what heinous sin is it in me*
To be ashamed to be my father's child!
But though I am a daughter to his blood,
I am not to his manners.'
She hates her father and the way he behaves, but she loves Lorenzo. 'Lorenzo,' she says to herself, '*if thou keep promise*, I will become a Christian and marry you.'

Having delivered Jessica's letter to Lorenzo, Launcelot returns to Shylock's house to tell him that Shylock has been invited to have supper with Bassanio. Launcelot also tells Shylock that there is to be a masquerade (masked) ball.

As Launcelot leaves, he gives Jessica the nod: '*Mistress, look out at window, for all this, There will come a Christian boy, will be worth a Jewess' eye.*'

He is telling her that Lorenzo has her letter and he will keep his promise.

Later, again at Shylock's house, Gratiano and Salarino are waiting for Lorenzo. They are dressed for the masquerade ball.

Lorenzo turns up, followed by Jessica, who has fled her father's house and is disguised as a boy. Lorenzo wants Jessica to be his torchbearer for the parade.

Lorenzo, Jessica and Salarino leave, just as Antonio arrives to tell Gratiano that there will be no masquerade ball tonight. But the wind is good, so Bassanio says he will head off to Belmont straight away. Gratiano will go with him.

Meanwhile, back in Belmont, it's time for the Prince of Morocco to choose one of Portia's caskets.

The gold casket has an inscription, 'Who chooseth me shall gain what many men desire.'

The silver casket carries the promise, 'Who chooseth me shall get as much as he deserves.'

The lead casket warns, 'Who chooseth me must give and hazard all he hath.'

'How do I choose?' asks the prince.

'One of the caskets has my picture in it,' explains Portia. 'If you get the casket with the picture in it, you get me too.'

The prince chooses the gold casket and

opens it. It contains no picture, but a skull with a scroll in its empty eye-socket.

The prince leaves empty-handed.

Salarino and Salanio are in the street, catching up on gossip. Salanio tells Salarino that he saw '*the villain Jew*' and '*the dog Jew*' (he means Shylock) shouting in the streets.

'He's found out that his daughter, Jessica, has run off with a Christian, Lorenzo. And Jessica has stolen money and jewels from her father. Shylock's not happy.

'Antonio had better pay his debt on time,' adds Salanio, 'or he will pay for this.'

Back at Portia's house, another suitor, the **Prince of Arragon**, has turned up to choose his casket. Portia explains the rules and shows him the caskets. (It's just like a TV gameshow.)

The prince chooses to open the silver casket – and he does see a picture inside. But it's not a picture of Portia. It's a picture of a *blinking idiot* holding up a scroll.

Prince Arragon too leaves empty-handed.

'The candle has singed another moth,' says Portia. 'When they make a choice, these men only know how to lose.'

Then a messenger arrives with news that a new suitor is about to arrive. The suitor is bringing expensive gifts, and the messenger is impressed by him:

'Yet I have not seen
So likely an ambassador of love.'
Ooo! Who can it be?

THREE

Salanio and Salarino are standing in a street in Venice. It's time for more gossip.

'It looks like Antonio's lost a ship,' says Salarino. 'It was shipwrecked in the English channel.'

Then Shylock turns up. He is still very upset about Jessica. '*My own flesh and blood to rebel!*' he tells Salanio.

Salarino changes the subject. 'Have you heard about Antonio's loss at sea?'

'That's another bad deal I've made!' Shylock says. '*He was wont to call me usurer* [money-lender]; *let him look to his bond: he* was wont to lend money for a Christian courtesy; let him look to his bond.'

'You won't take his flesh if he can't pay, will you?' asks Salarino. 'What's the point?'

'I'll use his flesh to bait fish,' Shylock replies. '*If it will feed nothing else, it will feed my revenge.*'

Shylock does not like Antonio. '*He hath disgraced me, and hindered me half a million; laughed at my losses, mocked at my gains,*

scorned my nation, *thwarted my bargains,
cooled my friends, heated mine enemies; and
what's his reason? I am a Jew.'*

Shylock goes on. '*Hath not a Jew eyes?
Hath not a Jew hands, organs, dimensions,
senses, affections, passions? fed with the same
food, hurt with the same weapons, subject to
the same diseases, healed by the same means,
warmed and cooled by the same winter and
summer, as a Christian is? If you prick us, do
we not bleed? if you tickle us, do we not laugh?
if you poison us, do we not die? and if you
wrong us, shall we not revenge?'*

Shylock's friend **Tubal** arrives. He has
been looking for Jessica, but, he tells
Shylock, he hasn't been able to find her.

'*I would my daughter were dead at my foot,
and the jewels in her ear!* She could be lying
in her coffin, with the jewels in the coffin
with her. Nobody has bad luck but me,'
Shylock responds.

'Antonio's had bad luck too,' says Tubal.
'A ship coming from Tripoli has been

31

wrecked. I hear that Antonio can't escape going bankrupt.'

Shylock is pleased at the bad news about Antonio. '*I am very glad of it: I'll plague him; I'll torture him: I am glad of it.* I will have his heart if he does not pay me back on time.'

Bassanio, Portia and Gratiano are at Portia's house. Bassanio has done his 'suitor' stuff and now it's time for him to choose a casket.

'Wait a day or two before choosing,' Portia begs him. 'If you choose now and choose wrongly, I will lose your company straight away.' (She obviously wants Bassanio to choose the right box.)

But Bassanio won't delay. He goes ahead and makes his choice.

He rejects the gold casket because it is too flashy. '*The world is still deceived with ornament … Hard food for Midas, I will none of thee.*'

He rejects the silver casket too, and chooses to open the lead casket. He looks inside, and there is Portia's picture. *Yes!* Bassanio has won his bride.

'Bassanio, everything I am and everything I have is now yours. *This house, these servants and this same myself*

Are yours, my lord.'

She gives Bassanio a ring, telling him that if he ever gives it away or loses it, their love is doomed.

Gratiano then announces his love for Nerissa. He tells Bassanio, 'I hope we can be married at the same time as you and Portia.'

Then Lorenzo, Jessica (*'his infidel'*) and **Salerio**, a merchant from Venice, arrive at the house. Salerio has a letter for Bassanio from Antonio.

Bassanio reads the letter. It is bad news. 'Portia,' Bassanio begins, 'when I told you I had nothing, I was actually bragging. In fact I have *worse than nothing*.'

He goes on to explain his arrangement with Antonio to borrow money – and now, this letter reports, Antonio has lost everything. All his business ventures have failed and he will not be able to repay Bassanio's debt to Shylock.

Salerio adds that, even if Antonio could repay the debt, Shylock would probably not take it. '*Never did I know*

A creature, that did bear the shape of man,

So keen and greedy to confound a man.'

Salerio says that Shylock is determined to get a pound of Antonio's flesh – the forfeit if he cannot repay the debt.

But Portia has a solution. 'He's owed three thousand ducats? That's all? Well, pay him six thousand and cancel the debt. I'll pay double or triple that, rather than let any friend suffer because of you, Bassanio. Now, come with me to get married, then you can go to Venice to see your friend.'

Simple.

Back in Venice, Shylock is with Salanio and Antonio.

'Shylock, listen … ' begins Antonio.

'I'm going to have my bond,' Shylock interrupts. *Thou call'dst me dog before thou hadst a cause;*

But, since I am a dog, beware my fangs.'

'Please, Shylock … '

'I'll have my bond; I will not hear thee speak:

I'll have my bond; and therefore speak no more.' Shylock is determined.

'I'm sure the duke won't enforce this contract,' says Salanio hopefully.

'The duke cannot deny the course of law,' replies Antonio. 'All trade in Venice depends on it. I've lost so much weight worrying about it all that there won't be a pound of flesh to give to *my bloody creditor.* I just hope Bassanio comes to see me pay his debt.'

Portia's house again. Bassanio has left for Venice with Portia's money, to try to sort things out.

Portia asks Lorenzo and Jessica to stay and look after her house until Bassanio comes back. She tells them that, until Bassanio returns, she is going to live in a monastery with Nerissa.

Then Portia gives a letter to her servant, **Balthazar**, to be delivered to her cousin **Bellario** in Padua. 'He will give you letters and clothes,' she tells the servant. 'Whatever he gives you, bring to the Venice ferry and meet me there.'

Portia has a plan!

But is it a cunning plan?

FOUR

The scene is a court of justice in Venice.
The **Duke of Venice** is there, together with
Antonio, Bassanio, Gratiano and Salarino.
Shylock is waiting outside.

The duke tells Antonio, '*I am sorry for
thee; thou art come to answer*

A stony adversary, an inhuman wretch
uncapable of pity, void and empty

From any dram of mercy.' He is talking
about Shylock. Obviously Antonio is not
the only one who doesn't like Shylock.

The duke has Shylock called in to the
court. 'Shylock,' the duke begins, 'everybody

thinks you are just pretending to be cruel.
I agree. They think you will change your
mind at the last minute and show mercy to
Antonio. What do you say? *We all expect a
gentle answer, Jew.*'

'You want to know why I prefer to have
my pound of flesh rather than three thousand
ducats,' answers Shylock. 'I'll not answer
that – but let's just say it's because I feel
like it. I can't give a reason and I won't

give a reason, other than the hate and loathing I feel for Antonio.'

'That's no answer,' says Bassanio.

'*I am not bound to please thee with my answers*,' replies Shylock.

'Bassanio, give it a rest,' says Antonio. 'Arguing with the Jew … you might as well stand on the beach and tell the tide to be lower. *Let me have judgment and the Jew his will*.'

Bassanio turns to Shylock. 'Here are six thousand ducats.'

'You can offer me six times that amount, and still I won't accept it. *I would have my bond*.'

The duke declares that he has sent for the legal expert Bellario to attend the court and give his views on the case. Bellario will act as judge and settle the matter.

Salerio then announces that a **messenger** has arrived from Bellario. The messenger is ushered in. It is in fact Nerissa, disguised as a lawyer's clerk. She hands the duke a letter.

As the duke reads the letter, Shylock begins to sharpen his knife on the sole of his shoe.

Gratiano quips bitterly, '*Not on thy sole, but on thy soul, harsh Jew,*

Thou makest thy knife keen.'

He then has a rather long and tedious go at Shylock.

'Unless you can undo my signature on the contract, you're just wearing out your lungs by all this talking. I stand here with the law on my side,' Shylock tells Gratiano simply.

The duke has read the letter. 'Bellario says he is sick at the moment, but he is sending a young lawyer from Rome, called **Balthazar**. They have discussed the case between them and Bellario is sending this young expert in his place. 'Is Balthazar here?' asks the duke.

Funnily enough, he's just outside.

Balthazar walks into the court. Guess what? It's Portia in disguise. This is her cunning plan.

'Antonio,' begins Balthazar/Portia. 'This man has a claim on you. Correct?'

'Yes.'

'Do you acknowledge the contract?'

'I do.'

'Then,' says Balthazar, 'the Jew must show mercy.'

'What? Why?' asks Shylock.

Cue that famous speech from Portia (disguised as Balthazar):

'The quality of mercy is not strain'd.
It droppeth as the gentle rain from heaven
Upon the place beneath.

'Mercy blesses the one who gives it and the one who receives it,' says Balthazar, 'and it is mightiest in the mightiest people. A king's sceptre represents his earthly power, but mercy is a higher power than that. Mercy is a quality of God himself. Earthly power comes closest to God's power when mercy is combined with justice.

'So, Jew,' Balthazar continues, 'justice is your plea, but consider this: Justice won't save our souls. We pray for mercy and this same prayer teaches us to show mercy too.'

Good speech!

Bassanio begs the duke to bend the law, just this once, but Balthazar says that can't be allowed.

Shylock stands firm. *'There is no power in the tongue of man*

To alter me: I stay here on my bond.'
He wants his pound of flesh.

Antonio demands the verdict of the court, and Balthazar gives it: *'Why then, thus it is:*

You must prepare your bosom for his knife.'
Balthazar tells Antonio to bare his chest – *'Nearest his heart,'* as the contract says. Balthazar asks Shylock to pay for a surgeon to stand by, *'To stop his wounds lest he do bleed to death,'* but Shylock refuses – that's not in the contract, so he won't pay for it.

'A pound of that same merchant's flesh is thine:

The court awards it, and the law doth give it,'

Balthazar tells Shylock. 'But wait a
moment. This contract does not allow you
to take any blood from Antonio. It only
allows you to take "*a pound of flesh*". If you
shed *one drop of Christian blood* when you
make the cut, all your lands and goods will
be confiscated by the state of Venice.'

Checkmate.

'Ah,' says Shylock. He thinks for a while.
'OK. I'll take your offer. Pay me six thousand
ducats and Antonio can go.'

'Oh no,' says Balthazar. 'The Jew has demanded his justice. *Therefore prepare thee to cut off the flesh.*

Shed thou no blood, nor cut thou less nor more

But just a pound of flesh.'

Balthazar is saying that, because Shylock refused the money and demanded his pound of flesh in court, he's not allowed now to change his mind and take the money instead. He must take his pound of flesh. Shylock will have justice and his penalty, and that's all he can have.

But, if Shylock cuts more or less than a pound of flesh, even by just a tiny bit, if the weighing scales change by just so much as a hair from exactly one pound, then Shylock will die and his goods will be confiscated.

Shylock makes to leave. 'I'm not staying here any more to argue with you.'

'One more thing,' says Balthazar. 'The laws of Venice say that if a foreign person attempts to kill any person, the person he tried to kill gets half of the foreigner's goods. The other half goes to the state of Venice. And whether the offending person is put to death as punishment or not – well, that's up to the duke.'

Balthazar continues. 'Shylock, you've clearly tried to take the defendant's life. So get down on your knees and beg for mercy before the duke.'

The duke immediately pardons Shylock, but says that half his wealth shall go to Antonio.

'What mercy can you render him, Antonio?' Balthazar asks.

'If the duke sets aside the fine for one half of Shylock's property,' says Antonio, 'then I'm happy – provided that he lets me have the other half of his property to give, upon his death, to Lorenzo, the man who stole his daughter. Plus … Shylock must immediately become a Christian, and he must make a will that leaves all his property to Lorenzo and Jessica when he dies.'

Shylock has no choice; he has to agree.
He agrees, then leaves the court.

There's relief all round in court. Bassanio
offers Balthazar the three thousand ducats
(Bassanio doesn't know that Balthazar is
really his wife Portia), but Balthazar
refuses.

Bassanio begs Balthazar: '*Take some*
remembrance of us, as a
tribute,

Not as a fee.'

So Balthazar asks Antonio for his gloves, which Antonio gives to him. Then Balthazar asks Bassanio for the ring he is wearing – the ring Portia gave him that he vowed never to lose. Bassanio tries to wriggle out of it, but Balthazar insists. '*I will have nothing else but only this.*'

Bassanio comes clean: 'This ring was given to me by my wife, and she made me vow I would never sell it, give it away or lose it.'

So Balthazar leaves without the ring.

But then Antonio tells Bassanio he should let Balthazar have the ring. So Bassanio gives it to Gratiano and tells him to run after Balthazar and give him the ring.

Outside in the street, Gratiano catches up with Balthazar and gives him Bassanio's ring. Nerissa (still in disguise) tells Balthazar that she will try to get her husband Gratiano's ring, which he too swore he would keep forever.

FIVE

Lorenzo and Jessica are looking after Portia's house, as they promised. One of Portia's servants arrives, to tell them that Portia will be returning from 'the monastery' before sunrise. Her maid will come with her.

Then Launcelot arrives to tell them that Bassanio will arrive in the morning.

Portia and Nerissa arrive back at Portia's house in Belmont. Both are no longer in disguise. Then Bassanio, Gratiano and Antonio all turn up.

Soon Gratiano and Nerissa are arguing about Gratiano's missing ring. Gratiano tells Portia it's just '*a hoop of gold, a paltry ring*

That she did give me.'

He tells Nerissa that he gave the ring to a boy, a little boy 'no taller than you' as a fee.

But Nerissa is unhappy; Gratiano had promised to wear it until the day he died.

Portia scolds Gratiano. 'To be fair, you've given your wife good reason to be upset. If it happened to me, I'd be very upset too!'

Gulp! Bassanio is looking on and feeling uncomfortable. He says to himself: '*Why, I were best to cut my left hand off*

And swear I lost the ring defending it.'

Then Gratiano spills the beans. 'Bassanio gave his ring away, too. He gave it to the lawyer – who actually did deserve it.'

Bassanio admits it, but Portia is not happy. 'Just as there's no ring on your finger, there's no truth in your heart. I will

never sleep in your bed until I see the ring again.'

'Same for me,' Nerissa tells Gratiano.

But Portia isn't satisfied yet. She tells Bassanio, 'Since that lawyer's got the ring I loved, the ring you swore to keep for me, that lawyer can come to my house. He can have everything.

I'll not deny him any thing I have,
No, not my body, nor my husband's bed.

And Bassanio, if you leave home, even

for one night, *I'll have that doctor for my bedfellow.*'

'*And I his clerk.*' Nerissa tells Gratiano.

They pause to let that sink in.

'It's all my fault,' says Antonio.

Portia gives Antonio a ring. 'Give my husband this ring, and tell him he'd better not lose it like the last one.

Antonio gives the ring to Bassanio, who looks at it. 'It's the same ring! What?'

'I got it from the lawyer,' says Portia. 'I had to sleep with him to get it back.'

Portia's going to milk this for all she can get!

Nerissa takes out her ring. 'And I slept with the lawyer's clerk to get this one back.'

Portia hands them a letter from Bellario. 'Read this. It explains everything. I was the lawyer, and Nerissa was my clerk.'

Bassanio and Gratiano look at each other and both let out a deep breath.

'We didn't recognise you!' gasps Bassanio.

Portia gives another letter to Antonio. 'Three of your ships have arrived safely in harbour, loaded with wealth. You have no money worries now.'

Gratiano looks at Nerissa. 'So you were the clerk who was going to cheat on me?'

Nerissa says, 'Yes, but the clerk will never do it, unless he grows up to be a man.'

Bassanio turns to Portia:

'*Sweet doctor, you shall be my bed-fellow:*
When I am absent, then lie with my wife.'

Then Portia gives Shylock's signed deed to Lorenzo and Jessica; when Shylock dies, they shall inherit everything he owns.

So it's good news all round and everybody is happy. Everybody has managed to get a good outcome in the end.

Except Shylock.

 **THE END**

What's the play about?

The Merchant of Venice is always identified as one of Shakespeare's comedies. In Shakespeare's time, 'comedy' meant a light-hearted play with a happy ending. Although there are amusing scenes in the play, it is the dramatic scenes that are best remembered.

The plot of the play itself really focuses on the loan that Shylock makes to Bassanio, guaranteed by Antonio. When Antonio is unable to repay the loan, Shylock seeks his 'pound of flesh', the penalty he must pay according to his agreement with Antonio.

The comedy parts of the play are mostly overshadowed now by the religious issues raised in the play, particularly the hatred between Christians and Jews (the latter represented in the play by Shylock).

This is a difficult topic, and even today people still debate whether Shakespeare himself was being anti-semitic in the play.

The answer, as is often the case with Shakespeare, is that his characters are usually complex and many-sided. It's true that Shylock has many unpleasant characteristics – and he does seek revenge against Antonio. But it's also true that the outcome of the dispute is not fair on him and it's difficult not to feel sympathy for his poor treatment.

Similarly, Antonio admits that he has behaved very badly towards Shylock in the past – and most likely will carry on doing so. Yet, in spite of that, he is willing to put his life on the line for his friend Bassanio.

What are the main themes in the play?

Love and hate – As in many Shakespeare plays, there are different kinds of love in this play. There is the love of friends (Antonio would give up his life for his friend Bassanio) and love within a family (Portia's respect for her father's wishes, even though he is dead).

There is also romantic love (between Bassanio and Portia, Gratiano and Nerissa, and Lorenzo and Jessica).

There is also a lot of hate in the play. This was a time when there was a lot of hate between Christians and Jews (for complex and historic reasons). This is reflected throughout the play.

There is also personal hatred between

Shylock and Antonio, made worse by religious hatred. This hatred drives Shylock to seek revenge, rather than simple payment, when Antonio cannot pay his debt to Shylock.

Mercy and justice – Portia's famous speech (as Balthazar) in the court focuses on the nature of mercy. She pleads with Shylock to show mercy on Antonio. Portia uses a Christian idea of mercy that comes from the New Testament: the idea of mercy as 'turning the other cheek'.

However Shylock sees justice as quite the opposite: 'an eye for an eye, a tooth for a tooth.' (His view is based much more on the teachings of the Old Testament.)

Shylock's claim against Antonio ends up in court, and the outcome of the case has many problems. Portia, in disguise as an unbiased lawyer, is in fact far from unbiased. Shylock does not get justice.

In the end, despite all her talk of showing

mercy, she shows Shylock no mercy. For all his faults, the cards are stacked against Shylock and in the end he loses almost everything (except his life).

In particular, at that time being forced to convert to Christianity would have been terrible for him to accept.

Appearance and reality – Many elements of the plot depend upon deceit: what appears to be the case is not really so. Portia and Nerissa both disguise themselves, fooling the court (and affecting the outcome of the case) and also fooling their husbands afterwards. Jessica too escapes by disguising herself as a man.

Shakespeare's words

Usually Shakespeare included both poetry and prose in his plays. Most of the time, characters of noble birth or who have a higher social status speak in blank verse (poetry). More 'common' characters speak in prose. In *The Merchant of Venice*, Shakespeare mixes poetry and prose in interesting ways.

* Most of the time, Shylock speaks in blank verse, but in Act 3 Scene 1, when he is very angry (his speech '*I am a Jew. Hath not a Jew eyes?*'), he speaks in prose. This is much more direct and has a powerful and dramatic effect on the audience, communicating his anger clearly.

A lot of the humour in the play comes from the characters playing with words (**word play**). In particular, there are lots of **puns**.

✻ More than once Shakespeare creates puns around the words 'gentle' and 'gentile' (meaning 'not Jewish'). For example, in the court scene, the duke says to Shylock, *'We all expect a gentle answer, Jew!'*

✻ Again in the court scene, Shylock sharpens his blade on the sole of his shoe. Gratiano says to him,
'Not on thy sole, but on thy soul, harsh Jew,
Thou makest thy knife keen.'
This is an obvious pun on soul/sole.